MADNESS FROM A BROKEN SOUL

MADNESS FROM A BROKEN SOUL

JAMAL CADOURA

ISBN-13: 9781793189981
ISBN-10: 9781793189981

Cover design and typesetting by Roseanna White Designs

Library of Congress Control Number: 2018675309
Printed in the United States of America

My heart returns to you. To the love that saved it. The love that set it free.

I don't know where you are now, but I know that my heart is your permanent residence. And if you ever need a place to stay, its doors are wide open. Its love awaits you.

—Jamal Cadoura

Part One:
The Breaking

All for you

Letting go was hard. I gripped the key close to my chest and stood frozen, until life shoved me forward and demanded that I set you free. Tears filled my eyes. Still, I walked to the future's gate. Unlocked it. Watched your shadow disappear.

Your footprints were the last things I saw. Your voice faded and the winds wrapped me in our memories. My body was a ship and my heart was its anchor. I couldn't move as pain choked me.

But I am content in knowing that I made the right choice. You deserve a better life. A more promising one. Full of the love and the adoration my hands and my lips failed to provide.

And when you find it, my heart will begin to rebuild. Though it pains me to say farewell, nothing will prevent me from wanting what's best for you. Even if it's not me.

Belated Gratitude

I took for granted the kind eyes that'd never let me leave their sight. The hands that'd toil hours over the stove to make me delicious, savory meals. The legs that'd walk upon any path I chose. And the mind that believed in me. I can't believe how foolish I was to neglect them.

I read something interesting today. It said that great relationships are built. Perhaps we're looking at great relationships as the sun: something that's been there since we opened our eyes, rather than a home: something we must build. Something we must pour hours of our time and our effort into.

I wonder if you and I could have built something. I tried to. But I felt marooned. While my hands were laying the bricks, yours were idling. You'd never give me the effort I required.

Maybe I didn't help. Maybe my short temper and my mood discouraged you. I bear blame, like we all do. I can't highlight your mistakes without acknowledging my own. I lather in them every night. Rinse nice and cold. Then, I watch our memories go down the drain.

An Engraved Pain

My departure awaited me, a predator outside in the dark. I didn't want to leave. I didn't want my feet to travel that pavement for the final time. If only the ground could have trapped me there. Away from the upcoming pain and sorrow. The heartache. The tears that would spend hours driving down the lanes of my face.

And all those lanes led to the same place: a detour away from the life I had known for four years. Years that saw me transform from a cub into the head of a pride. Years that brought a new home to you and the breakup of your family. Years that have planted seeds of pain in my heart.

I can't wait for these flowers to bloom, so that I can pick them and give them to my future healed self. I still hurt when I reminisce. My heart bleeds and my mind begs to be liberated from memory's oppression. The sky will be so much brighter when it's not smeared with this pain.

A Letter to My Ex:

No. This isn't a condemnation. I'm not going to vent about the ways she hurt me. Or the ways she kicked me out and made me feel worthless.

Because there were none of those moments. Actually, she was great to me. She treated me far better than anyone else did. Making sure I ate. That I had the best apparel for work. That I was in good spirits. And for those reasons, she deserved better.

Now, I'm going to speak directly to her:

I hope, with every fiber in me, that you forgive me. And more than that, I hope you're happy. Genuinely, sincerely happy. You deserve to be. I never left because you were bad to me. I left because, I didn't see us together in the future. I saw life taking you in one direction and me in another. Not all paths can converge. And I didn't want you forcing yourself to be somewhere that'd lead to unhappiness. To arguments and long nights of fighting. To frowned faces and tear-filled eyes.

I was incapable of loving you in the ways that you deserve. Your love was all-encompassing, the night's shadow that covers the Earth. But my love was a small pond. Maybe we comforted ourselves and prolonged the departure by naively believing that a storm would come and transform the pond into a lake.

But I knew better. My feelings, and my desires, were decaying. They had become an old dwelling with mold and chipped wood. And I didn't want the house to collapse on you. I didn't want you to become a casualty.

You deserve hands that can hold you in the ways mine failed to. A strong body that will fulfill your need to rest as mine walked away. Legs that will approach you, and your qualities, with more fervor than mine did. I left so you could obtain all that. So you could be shown your worth.

It is cruel to stay in a place simply to preserve our emotions. If the preservation of my emotions was going to cost you your happiness, I needed to suspend them.

And I did. I am away because new opportunities need to step in and take my place. New love can enter and clothe you and your body that houses an infinite amount of kindness. And I can't wait to know that you're happy. That you're contented because you've received the love, and the joy, that I couldn't provide.

I am thankful for the memories. The times we'd laugh together and get ice cream as the world dozed off. The times I was able to express parts of me that I was too afraid to share with anyone else.

Where pain is found, love and happiness are beneath it. It is sad that it ended. But it is beautiful to know that you, my dear, will receive the smile, the warmth, and the adoration that you deserve. I am wishing you the best, always.

A Love that Never was:

I regret making those poor choices. Choices that led to agony. But we overcame them. Don't you remember? We were shown the beauty of communication. That, with a few words and a willingness to fight, we could bury those problems. Place a tombstone over their graves and smile at one another.

But now, you are reluctant. You are a shooting star and I am the earth. I will only be allotted a few glances of you. Of this potential. Of the secrets I couldn't wait to unearth beneath your soft, tender skin. Yet I am resigned to a fate without you. A life devoid of your love.

The moments I coveted have become the moments I regret having. They've shown me the sweetness of forever. Ran their hands along the strings of my heart. It destroys me knowing that I cannot savor your sweetness anymore. But I cannot fight a war that you won't send me to. That's a job for another soldier.

Wishing You the Best

I saw that you moved into a new house. I hope it's warmer. Kinder. Offering better memories, and better company, than your previous home did. The one that your family left. The one that your cruel uncle settled into.

I remember walking down those creaking stairs, carrying boxes full of lamps, bedsheets, and sorrow. The same stairs that absorbed your gleeful footsteps upon your family's purchase, were the same stairs that guided us to your departure. To a new chapter in your life. A moment where everything around you crumbled.

I began thinking about us. The future. My desires. The time we had spent. And I realized that I could no longer be there. The pain was unbearable. Guilt was consuming me. I needed to be the final part of your old life that left. That completely decimated itself. To create new space for you. New areas for a better love, and a better person, to enter.

We cry and affix sentiments to old items, like couches, TVs, and beds. But we forget how rejuvenating it is to get new ones. So, don't cry over me. I'm unworthy of your tears. Rejoice in my departure. It's your chance to get everything you're worthy of.

Remember Me

The hardest part is seeing that people are happier without us. We are the leaves that stroll by their feet. They'll occasionally step on us. But nothing will register. They move on. Making new friends. Taking longer hikes. Going to new places. And we recede in the background.

Perhaps this is why I pay attention to the smaller things. Like the snow that melts as warmth approaches. Even if its time was short, I want it to know that someone appreciated it. The way I'd want someone to remember and appreciate me.

An Improper Goodbye

I wanted to give you a proper goodbye. I left way too soon. A warplane flying away from the land it just bombed. You were an innocent bystander, staring into the flying debris and the decimated foundations. I'm sure they were littered with pictures of us. Like the pictures I had at home above my fireplace.

It's crazy, isn't it? To realize that you and I shared years together. That you and I helped one another grow. And that you and I are now one another's biggest lesson.

A Harsh Realization

I regret not enjoying you more. Not fully immersing myself in your inner greatness. It came in a small package. A quiet tone. A tiny frame. A peaceful manner. Your lips never spewed venom. Your voice never touched the ceiling.

I miss you. In everything. I find your smile peering at me in the menus of restaurants we'd frequent. In the racks of familiar clothing stores. I hear your voice in the background of songs that we'd blare in our cars. I see you everywhere.

And I'm waiting to see myself. To let go of the pain chaining me to the past. I want to look ahead and open the door. The future is coming. And I need to be ready.

The Pain of Letting Go

My cheeks are glass windows and my eyes are rainy skies. You are on the other side of the glass. I can see you. I can hear your voice faintly. But I cannot touch you.

I smash my fists against the windows. No response. The future prevents me. He tells me that you no longer have a place in my life, nor I a place in yours.

And nothing hurts more than knowing that two hearts still care about one another, but that they must depart. That they must embark on new journeys, so that each individual can get what they deserve.

It's Always Remembered

There may be heartache. There may be pain. Tears. Scrunched faces and agony. But there is also love. A love that fixed us. That taught us who we are and what we're composed of. That taught us how to enjoy the moment. How to walk without worries of the future. It was there.

And we felt it. I felt it. I felt you. My soul sprung with joy as my head rested upon your heartbeats. It was a beautiful symphony, a tune of forever.

Wishing it Could Have Been Different

I think about my mother. I reminisce on the moments that collapsed. When I was a child, she was my best friend. This is a new admission. An admission that's setting my pain free.

We would do everything together. Take walks. Go out to eat. Visit my aunt and my cousins. On Fridays, I'd look forward to us going out to a nice restaurant, and then heading out to see a movie, or to visit some relatives.

I still recall the uninhibited elation I experienced on one of those Fridays. I was sitting in the lunch room, eating chips and joking with my friends. I was exhilarated for the clock to strike 2:55. For the bell to ring and liberate us all into the weekend's arms. My mother and I were going to Famous Dave's that day. I relished the ribs and the cornbread. I couldn't wait.

I reflect on these times and I wonder why we grew so distant. Why we couldn't sustain the enjoyment of one another's presence. Why she had to turn to pills and succumb to agony. Why I had to succumb to my anger. The wrath that forced insults and obscenities out of my throat. I do seek forgiveness. From myself, above anyone. That was not the man I wanted to be. I have learned from those mistakes.

But for some peculiar reason, I cannot release myself from these inner shackles. I cannot set myself in her presence. It fills me with unease. With regret and rage. I cannot accept that she is not the version I was accustomed to as a child. Indeed, things change and evolve. Old skins are shed and newness covers the surface. But her new self is comprised of complaints and negativity. She is a shadow of her former self, existing in darkness. Her words no longer provide the humor that'd draw my laughter. Instead, they pull on the strings of my sorrow. I want to overlook these things. I want to mend our relationship. Repair the broken pieces of the bridge so that happy feet can walk upon it once again. But I cannot rebuild with broken pieces. Pieces that ache for a past that's long gone. Pieces that remind me of all the hurt that was inflicted.

Practicing Forgiveness

And as these tears
fall,
I realize that I haven't
forgiven myself.
This pain, this suffering.
It won't go
away.
I am a cemetery
with too many
ghosts
to face.

Too Bad it Fell Apart

I no longer cry. What's done is done. I cannot change anything. My tears will not fertilize your return. Your feet have long left the ground that my eyes have rained upon.

But I still think about you. And I hope that, wherever you've ended up, you're happy.

A Selfless Love

If I've ever let you go, it's not because I didn't love you. It's because I loved you so much, that I needed to set you free to obtain what you're worthy of.

A Prisoner to The Past

Goodbyes linger. Like a man on a cliff. Like the last petal on a flower. Like the sun as it dips slowly into the horizon. And I'm left wondering when I'll smile at the incoming hellos. When I'll rise and laugh again.

The seasons change, but the sadness remains. Regret accompanies me into every room, offering a formal introduction: hi. My name is Jamal. You may see the smile on my face, but my sad eyes reflect a past that still has its claws in my back. My ears hear the echo of her voice. My neck twists whenever I drive by her old place, hoping to catch a glimpse of her, or the cat, in the window.

But she is no longer there. Nor are the memories. Nor is the desire. Only my brokenness remains. The sharp pieces that slice through my flesh.

A Restless Mind

My mind is a room with windows. I see numerous things. My ex roaming the horizon, a new lover holding her hands; my grandmother searching through the broken pieces of her past, wondering where she went wrong; my mother, older and enfeebled, with tears streaming down her face, her hands sifting through my old photos carefully, as if they are shards of glass. I go to open the windows. I want to yell and save them.

But they're locked. So, I stay inside, watching with weeping eyes. With a wilting heart and a dwindling desire. No matter how many times my heart rebuilds, something is always waiting to break it.

The War Within

Some days,
it is hard
to make peace
with the decisions
I went to war with.

No Rest for the Active Mind

I admire those who can "live in the moment." Those who can suspend their inhibitions and laugh as doom awaits. Those who do not need perfection, but a bit of sunshine and green grass. An ocean's breeze and a colored sky.

I've tried living in the moment. I've tried ignoring my worries. Tucking them into dark places and saying that we can discuss this later. But when things matter to me, they must be addressed immediately. I cannot risk disvaluing them or hurting them.

So, I am robbed of enjoying the moment. I am prevented from unwrapping the gifts that the present hands out. I'm busy painting the skies with my worries. Looking into the future with scared eyes and a troubled mind. I mull over all the things that could go wrong and all the impending heartache. It's a plague I haven't found the cure for.

A Haunting Goodbye

We talked about ending it. And after that, you still told me to finish the delicious food that you made. Even after I buried the coffin, your last wish was that I leave the cemetery full. How can I repay such kindness and love? Maybe you didn't tell me you loved me, but you showed it in so many ways. For that, I am eternally grateful. Perhaps that is why my hand still clings to the door of your home as my feet trek across the pavement. I'm going to end up tearing myself in two.

I will never forget leaving that house for the last time. Heaviness clung to my heart and tears pooled in my eyes. I was walking away from an innocent soul who deserved more than I could give. Away from the pavement where we once walked together as we filled the inside with groceries. Where we'd laugh and would sneak the cat in because it was against the apartment's policies.

I rushed to my car for fear that my tears would escape and populate her lawn. Once inside, I bawled my eyes out. I was an inconsolable child who had been ripped away from the life, and the best friend, he'd always known. But I did the right thing. I set a great woman free, and onto the path to get what she deserves.

And someday, I'm going to tell this story to someone in a similar situation. And I'm going to set two other great people free, and onto the path to get what they both deserve.

Part Two:
The Healing

Grace, Dear Friends

Don't hate them. Don't wish misfortune upon them. I understand you're hurting. You're picking up the pieces that they shattered. But people don't always leave us out of malice and cruelty.

Sometimes, our paths must diverge, and we must embark on separate journeys. But it doesn't negate the beauty that existed. The smiles, the laughter, and the growth that was shared. There is still so much to be thankful for. And these lessons will carry us to greater heights with new lovers and new memories.

It's All Connected

Your emotions aren't chalk; time isn't an eraser. Face them. Don't wish for their nonexistence. They are the very aspects that make you the great person you are. With joy, comes pain; with happiness, comes sadness; and with celebration, comes mourning.

All things are inextricably intertwined, as the rain is to the same skies that bestow sunlight. The very emotions that make you feel depths of sadness, are also the same emotions that make you feel endless love.

Hang in There

Your heart is broken. But it's still beating. It's still carrying your dreams. The future is also alive. And though you can't see it now, it's beckoning to you.

Brighter days are ahead, where the heartache will be quieter. A distant voice in the winds. You'll tread upon the old memories occasionally—but with a smile. And the happiness you'll feel, will be an evolution of the sadness you have overcome.

Your Perspective is Key

Saying goodbye will rip your core. As you walk away, memories will tug at your feet and beg you to stay. You'll recall the moments of laughter and the times that love hung heavy in your heart.

But you can't focus on the past. There's a reason you must leave. Your path must go elsewhere, so that you can find what you're truly seeking. And instead of focusing on what you're leaving behind, you need to invest yourself into everything you're building. The lessons you've learned, and the memories you've made, will allow you to forge a life that's meant for your fullest depths.

We All Heal Differently

Don't place a timetable on your healing. Don't compare the way others have healed, to the way you're still struggling. You are a universe of intricacies; you will absorb and react to tragedies differently than others.

There is no shame in the way your heart breaks. It shows that you're a deep, wondrous human, with an infinite amount of depth.

Cry. Yell. Sulk. But make sure that you don't condemn yourself. Healing takes a while, and you deserve your own kindness. You will get there eventually, through grace and compassion. And you must honor your broken parts along the way.

It's All Normal

Pain doesn't mean that you made the wrong decision. Nor does it mean that you must return. It's normal to grieve all losses. You have every right to be hurt. Let your heart shatter; let your tears fall.

But you must remember the reasons you made a decision. Hurt can't change that. And returning is worse. You'll never be able to build the future you deserve.

The Other Side

Be patient with her. It's not always about you. You are not the center of her world, nor are you the reason for her silence and her suffering. She is a universe of varying emotions and struggles; sometimes, she needs to close her doors to recover. To heal. To gather herself for tomorrow's battles.

Be there for her. Let your arms be the strong oak trees she can rest her weary head against; let your words be the sweet remedies that'll coax her problems away. And when she needs space, be a traveler. Go to another part of her world temporarily. When it's time for you to return, she'll arrange your flight.

But don't blame yourself, and don't fight with her. It's not about you. It never was. She is her own individual, and if you're going to love her, you must love everything that she is.

You're Normal

You're not crazy. Whatever you're going through is normal. Dealing with the pain of a breakup? It's normal. Scared to start the gym or a new job? It's normal. Wondering about someone from the past? It's normal. All of it is normal.

You're human. You have hundreds of thoughts and emotions coursing through you. You're going to be a mess at times and you're going to struggle. Don't be hard on yourself and don't stay down. You will get through this, and you will see that, though this journey is messy, it's still enjoyable. And we can make the most of it.

It's Time to Let Go

I can't tell you how to heal. But I can tell you that you don't need to carry this weight. Toss it out. Let the winds rush through your hair and empty it of all worries and fears. You don't need to hang onto "what-ifs" and cling to edges that people, and opportunities, have long left. Look up at the sky, marvel at the sun, and know that a better love awaits you.

Never Surrender Who You Are

Struggling to move on doesn't mean you're "weak." It's a testament to your big heart and to your humanity. You genuinely bond with others and you value their presence.

You're deep. Not shallow and forgetful, like many other cold individuals. You have a warm inside, and you should never extinguish those inner flames. Keep your big heart and your sincere emotions. You may feel things far more deeply than others. And that's OK. You will also kindle the most genuine connections and the purest love.

Always and Forever

Warmth enveloped my body, and nerves ran through my veins. Finally, you emerged. Glowing, drawing my attention and absorbing all the light around us. An angel descending from the heavens, coming to rescue the lost and the broken. When we got to the venue, I was engrossed in our conversation. Hundreds of people were around, laughing and moving, but my eyes were fixed on you. My heart couldn't stop smiling and my mind fumbled for the right words. If only I could make you feel as beautiful, and as lovable, as you are in my head.

And here's a secret. Each time you were in front of me, I wanted to lean into the back of your hair and inhale its scent. I needed something to take home with me. A piece of you I could lock away in my memory and protect. A piece that would encapsulate the perfection embodied in you and that memorable summer night. You are the gem and I am the case: I will protect you and allow your shine to emanate from within me. Awe is all you will ever know.

You are the Earth itself. I want to traverse all your countries. Show me your land of love. Your land of heartache and pain. Your land of misery. I will walk through them, wide-eyed and jubilant, scribbling notes in my book.

Show me your crevices and hidden caves. I want to run my hands through your secrets and through the hieroglyphics of your past. I will learn everything I can about you. There will never be a day where you'll have to explain yourself to me. I am a part of you, and you're safe with me. Everything about you will be guarded. And if there are areas I'm barred from, I will wait until you approve my visa. I am here until death's hands rip me away. And even then, my memory and my spirit shall live within you.

It Wasn't Personal, and I'm Sorry

I think about you and our old life. The couch that's empty. The cat sleeping atop it. Your tiny fingers traversing the remote to find a new show to occupy your mind.

I'd try to fill the fridge with fruits, vegetables, and meats. I'd try to fill the air with jokes and laughter. But the house remained empty. And that emptiness began to prey on me. I was deteriorating, an old rock being weathered by a storm. Pieces of me were falling off the cliff. I had to escape before the storm consumed what remained. I had to salvage myself. You became an unfortunate casualty in this internal war.

But I had to do what was best for me. I hope you can forgive me. And someday, when our hearts mend, we can talk about this and express ourselves. Pour our emotions out and fill containers with our sorrow. Until then, I am waving at you from afar and wishing you the best.

I Needed to Choose Me

You visit me sometimes. As if you're a spirit who hears my heart's calling. It wonders how you're doing. What your hair color is now. How you've been eating lately. What new lover whispers in your ears. Perhaps I'm unworthy of such knowledge. After all, I left when you needed me.

But I needed me. I needed to find my way. The path was darkening and the flowers inside my heart were dying. I could only bloom elsewhere. Away from the life I was comfortable in.

Still, I'd like to visit parts of my old life. But if I return to the people and the places I left, I'll never move forward.

I Only Wanted to Love You

I am so tired of loving you from afar. I want to cross your borders. Give me a visa. Stamp my passport with your symbol of love. Let me trek into your country and explore you. Let me taste your fruits of compassion. Let me swim in your rivers of joy. Let me run my hands across the ancient tales etched into your heart's walls. Let me understand you for all that you are.

Do not fear me. I am not a thief. Nor am I an invader. I am a curious traveler who has finally found what he's been searching for. And you, my dear, are the prophecy. The love that was promised to me. The woman that has fulfilled every desire roaring in my heart. The desires that howl during midnight and claw through my chest.

Let me in. Let me love you. Let my adoration safeguard your feelings. I will be the border that will protect this beautiful country. And together, we will create a kingdom of love.

I Love You for You

I love your brokenness. I find myself in each of your pieces. This piece speaks of heartache. It cuts deeply. I know its voice well. The way it whispers nightly. The way it masquerades as old lovers and as happier times.

This piece speaks of pain. When you had high hopes that someone would change. Only to walk into a room and see the same look in their eyes. The same wandering hands creating more trouble.

This piece speaks of fear. It makes you watch movies of all your failures. It laughs at you. Says that you're not enough. That people would be better off without you.

But all of these pieces still comprise a great you. A woman worthy of love. Tenderness. Affection. And when you're ready to open your gates, my love will rush in. It will fill your plains. Flowers will populate the ground. New travelers will come and stare in awe of everything that you are. And you will finally understand that you have always been a gem amongst the masses.

And Still, I Wonder

"What could have been." That statement lingers. A person dangling on a cliff. My heart wants to know what we could have built. But it doesn't matter now. Not when you're away. Not when you neglect all the beauty around you.

Like our enjoyment of one another. The nights in Downtown Detroit, coffee's scent permeating the air. A smile paved through your cheeks. The dim sky sending its cool breeze. We could have had more of those.

But you went away. Just as your heart's gates were opening, you slammed them shut and locked them. The least you could do is face me. Show me those eyes one last time. Let me look into them. I want to uncover if any of this was real. Is it really that easy to walk away? To no longer feel? I'm unsure.

But I am sure of my love for you. I was willing to fight. I still am. A knight suiting up to reclaim his kingdom. You are my kingdom. The place where the sun never sets. Where towers of love gaze upon me. And where potential roams endlessly.

Thank You, Daniel Caesar

That night was perfect. As perfect as God's hand would script it. I stayed in my car, awaiting your arrival. My stomach was in a knot, and my heart was fluttering. Birds were flying over the parking structure. I watched them soar into the skies, where they'd get a glimpse of your car pulling in before I did. My nerves rose and my inner panic button was pressed. I didn't want my mind to do what it always does on dates: overthink. I engrossed myself in a podcast. But in the back of my mind, you were approaching. Waiting to beckon me over. An invitation for us to continue exploring this land of love. The borders are unfamiliar to me; I'm unaccustomed to traveling such lands with fruitful abundance. Lands that dangle potential before my eyes.

Eventually, you arrived. I exited my car, my eyes frantically searching for you. You were nowhere to be seen. I walked around the parking garage, hoping your scent would guide me to you. And just as my frustration brewed, black pants and a blue jean jacket appeared around the corner. I couldn't muster the courage to tell you how beautiful you looked. How, upon the sight of you, my heart becomes the world's finest musician, writing songs about your dimples, your freckles, and your effervescent smile. I wanted to take your hand in mine. Caress your fingers with kindness and care. I wanted my touch to implant love in your skin. To allow adoration to cover your veins, the way winter's frost covers a river.

Eventually, we walked into the venue. People were packed around the stage's floor. I was in awe of the great blue arches and the golden carvings in the ceilings. I saw a statue of a knight in a corner, dressed in silver steel armor with a spear. It reminded me of who I become when I'm around you. A warrior, fighting for your love. Fighting for your protection. Fighting for your happiness.

A smile is the only thing I want to cross those cheeks. Cheeks that my lips yearn to press themselves against. Cheeks that blushed at the sight of the rose I gave you on our first date.

And you topped it off. Your natural beauty resonates through any building you're in. I hope I make you feel safe and loved. Appreciated and protected. I will always lift you, a throne lifting a queen.

I Love the Real You

I know you have a passion for life. A passion that I admire. My heart watches and stares in awe. You pass through horizons fiercely, a shooting star heading toward infinity.

But there is a fear in you. A voice you're trying to escape. It whispers secrets about the past. You take walks, visit new places, and engage in deep conversations because you're running. You don't want to face it. You don't want it to bury you.

But it won't. I am here for you. You can come to me when the voice grows too loud. When you can't hear yourself in the background. I know how hard it is to suffer in this unrelenting world. I will not let you suffer alone. I will turn my strength into water and pour it over you. My compassion will be a bed that you can rest in. I'll run my fingers through your hair, kiss your forehead, and tell you everything will be OK. You can rest easily, knowing that, when you awake, I'll still be here. Holding your hand through it all. Nudging you along the path when you feel your legs give out. And loving you unconditionally, no matter what storm arises.

I'm Here Forever

No storms will keep me away. No darkness is too much. I am here for the long run. Even if it means losing much of myself in the process. Time has shown me that I'm strong enough to rebuild. I always do. I pick up one brick of pain after another, and I build a home of love.

And I want you to reside within it. I want us to paint the walls with our story. Add portraits of our dates to every room. I want the floors to whisper with the excitement that our feet walk with whenever they approach one another. I want us to recline in the couches and express our feelings. I understand your emotions are deep streams. I will be the net that will capture unwanted debris. I will show you that you're worthy of the love you run from.

My love is yours. No matter how far you roam, it will find you. Guide you back to you. Restore you to your former glory. This home is ours. We will give birth to our new selves. We will tuck our sorrows in the attic. We will build anew every day the sun rises and spreads its wings through our bedroom. As the light dances between your long, flowing hair, I will kiss your cheeks. Pull you closer to me. Whisper that you are everything. That you are beautiful, irrespective of me. Irrespective of your struggles. I will remain in awe of your elegance. I want my adoration of you to be transcribed on my tombstone. I am many things in this life, but being your lover is foremost.

Don't Be Scared, My Love

Your past isn't any of my concern. Unless you want to tell me. If you are ever ready to take my hand and walk me through it, I will be there. Holding you tightly. Kissing your cheeks as tears run down them. Wiping your eyes clean and showing them your beauty instead of your pain. The strength in my heart is yours. And we will conquer your demons together.

I Was Right

Meeting you has been bittersweet. You have given me an unprecedented love. A love that fills my soul, the way heaven's rainfall fills the oceans. A love that has halted my internal bleeding. That lassos me away from bloodthirsty demons.

But you also came with many realizations. Realizations that destroyed my reality. You shattered many of my facades. I realized that I was in the wrong relationship and that I was coasting through life. I had to change. I had to better myself to be the man you need. It has all been so painful. And I'm uncertain of what you feel. If I'll ever claim your love and wear the crown beside you. Or if I'll be sent away.

Yet my heart knows the answer. You will end up departing. I will watch from sorrow's shores as your ship sails into a fading horizon and a dark sky. Thunder will roar, expressing the sadness my heart refuses to. The sadness that will haunt me like a ghost. That will chase every new endeavor away.

I don't know what my life would be like had I never met you. A part of me wishes I could see it. But it's too late. I have fallen for you. I find happiness in your freckles. I see the future in your eyes. They are the crystal balls that tell me that, years from now, I will still be chasing your heart. Begging for its affection. Yearning to hold it close, and to tell it that it's the finest jewel and my body is its chest. I find love in your smile. It's the manifestation of everything I've ever looked for. When I stare at you or converse with you, the world is a blur. You become the sun, giving light to those in darkness.

I hope this will work. I hope my thoughts will leave. That my future will decimate my worries, and that I'll find your smile in the wake of their destruction.

A Truthful Poem

If I seem
incomplete,
it's because I've left
pieces
of myself
in every
goodbye
I've ever experienced.

Thankful for Everything

Even if we must say goodbye, it is only to our bodies. Our spirits roam in another realm. Where the love is returned. Where the memories play in the sunlight, gleaming smiles on their faces. Where hands interlace and rise above pain's ashes.

Even if we must say goodbye, my heart will constantly wave to the better times across love's border. They are there. Giggling and skipping through the winds. And though our hearts break, we can find solace in the quiet moments where nothing mattered but the love on our lips and the sincerity in our eyes.

Always Trying to Love Her

She doesn't see the real me. I'm so engrossed in the journey of claiming her love, that I'm always in my armor. My sword is out, slicing through her doubts. Slicing through my own apprehensions. My helmet is on, hiding my mischievous smile and my fun-loving eyes. She doesn't see who I really am. She sees a warrior.

And while she may respect that, she is missing out on my other qualities. The qualities that could show her that I am flirtatious. That I am fun, enjoyable, and adventurous. That I have a child in me who wants to take her hand and roam freely through the mountains and along the shores. I have to show her these things. I am a lover. But I am also so much more.

Peeling the Layers

You always talk about "peeling the layers." I laugh at the way your hands peel an invisible onion when you say it. There is a hint of humor. But we both know it's much deeper. You like to delve deeply into people's inner oceans. You swim in the depths of their hearts to uncover all the treasures.

I'm waiting for you to swim in my heart. Find it. Knock on its doors. And when it answers and welcomes you in with your favorite coffee (one cream and two sugars), take a seat and begin peeling its layers. You will see the many truths I harbor, but do not reveal, because of fear.

My depths run deeply; I don't want you to drown. You're adventurous, but my feelings are not your average hike or your simple beach run. They are the roughest terrain with many hidden monsters. But once you surpass the monsters, you will find the hidden springs. Fairies will rise and sing the truths my heart holds for you. They will tell you all about your beauty. The way my eyes get lost in yours. The way my fingers want to trace and count every freckle on your dimpled cheeks. The way my legs will walk to the edge of the Earth and dive in, if that's what you request. Peel these layers and discover the true realms of love. And even if you run away after, I will be satisfied in knowing that I loved you the way you deserve to be loved.

What Love Should Be

How beautiful it is
to find someone
who loves you
for everything that you are
and for everything
that you're not.

A Gentle Reminder

It will get better. Your heart will heal. You will smile again. And you will rise to fight for what you deserve.

The Universe May Have Been Right

I feel you in every sad piano melody, as if the keys are aching for something. The way I ache for you. You have become such an important part of my life. But your detachment prevents you from bonding with me.

Maybe it's better that way. Maybe the universe is preventing a bond because it doesn't want to make our inevitable departure harder. I don't know. But even if you walk away, this was the closest to love I've gotten. And though it'll pain me to wave farewell, my heart will smile in knowing that love exists.

At Least I Learned Something

I wish I would have appreciated you more. But I couldn't then. My mind had too many roadblocks that appreciation couldn't drive through. My departure was the construction team that cleared them.

Next time, I'll do things differently. I'll live with more love. More openness. I won't miss a moment to bask in the glory of who my lover is. To cherish every waking second time has given me to hold her hands, to kiss her lips, and to share warm memories.

Value Your Heart

Yes, you shed tears. But at least you know your heart isn't numb. It's full of love. And this love will save so many. This love will set people free.

The Lesson I learned the Hard Way

Sometimes, we must accept that we are only people's experiences. We're meant to take them from one part of their journey to another. We are the steps they walk upon to reach new heights. The canyons they see along a rough path. They'll stop, exit, and marvel with wide eyes at our beauty. They'll occasionally tell others about us.

But they'll never come back. We will be relegated to the deepest parts of their memories. We can only enjoy the time allotted to us. Even if it means suppressing our inner voice that begs for more.

Maybe I'll Never Understand

It is strange watching people, and promises, fade into memories. Into worn books with tattered pages. I will never understand how time can be so fickle. How fate can be so cruel. We are granted people who we adore spending time with. We grow with them, laugh with them, and become accustomed to their habits. We surprise them with their favorite ice cream flavors and flowers. We take them on random dates to new parks and new paths.

And then, months later, we trek these paths alone. Fate decided that we had to part ways, and that we must coexist with only their memories in our hearts. But how can our hearts—these fragile, little things—carry such huge burdens? How can we move forward with the weight of the world on our shoulders?

But the Memories are Still Here

When you leave, take everything. Even these memories. Cherish them and remember me. I don't want to be forgotten. I want to know that I'm etched into your mind, and that you will carry pieces of me eternally.

Because I will carry pieces of you. I will remember the first moment you walked into the coffee shop, butterflies filling my stomach. I will remember the way my eyes spoke long before my mouth did: "Damn. She's beautiful." The way I wanted to place my arm around your shoulders as we strolled around downtown Detroit, the sunlight gleaming atop buildings.

I will remember walking into our first Lions game, your eyes widening like a newborn seeing the world for the first time. Blue jerseys were populating the hallways, but I only saw you. Your hair spilling down your shoulders, your freckles miniature stars existing on a galaxy of a woman I never tire of exploring. A woman who continuously inspires me and shows me what life is all about.

The War Destroyed My Home

Loving you is like living in a warzone. I never know when the bombs will drop and destroy everything I've built. I never know when the words "we're better as friends" are going to march in and give me an evacuation notice.

When you do come around, I never know if I should lower my heart's gates, or raise them higher. If I should have a "give this one more chance" affixed to my lips, or a "thank you for a great time today." You've redefined the term "living on the edge."

And I'm tired of being on the edge. Either you pull me up, or you let me tumble down. Being here is painful, and I deserve the love, the praise, and the joy I shower you in.

I Felt it Coming

I am mourning a loss that hasn't yet transpired. I feel your impending departure in my bones. I sense it, the way the birds sense winter's arrival. But I'm not heading elsewhere. I'm staying right here, and loving you until the end.

Until every last piece of my heart shatters and the universe tells me that it's time to move on. Yet even then, I will still keep you in my heart. I will still yearn for many things: a moment to kiss your sweet, smiling lips; a chance to hold you in my arms as the stars whisper their secrets; and a long walk where I can fully tell you how much I admire you and desire you, only to hear your acceptance at the end.

We're All One

Your past is dirty. So what? None of us are clean. We all have blemishes, and we all wear thicker clothes to hide our scars.

But we shouldn't. Our scars are the relics that attest to our greatness. We have survived odds we thought we never would, and here we are, offering inspiration to others. Lighting flames along the path to guide them home.

It's Still Early

Don't walk away. Not yet. Not as the sun of our love was just beginning to rise. Not as the horizon was starting to carve our story in it. Not as the neighbors were preparing to welcome us into love's neighborhood.

There's still so much left to see and do. Stay here and experience this journey with me. Set your eyes on the beautiful paths with multi-colored flowers in the distance. Watch as the wind brushes through us and molds our beings into one. As the universe smiles at its next greatest story. As the world bows and says that this, all inhabitants, is what love is: a partnership; a journey; a tale involving growth and determination. This is us. This is what we could be.

The Memories Hurt

I think about you. More often than I should. We were best friends. I caught your tears numerous times. You listened to me vent, and break down, numerous times. Those memories are seared in my mind. They do not fade.

They are the heirlooms people bring from their homelands. We keep them in glass containers and we only discuss them when someone questions. Even then, we downplay it.

"What's that picture?" someone will ask.

"Oh," we'll reply casually, feigning indifference, "that was something from my younger days. A good experience. So, did you see the game last night?"

"What's that trophy in your heart's vault?" another will ask, noticing its gleam from a distance. The tiny speckles of light that escape through the creases of the vault's door whenever we speak about our past loves. Our tones always betray us.

"Oh, that was from someone I used to date a while ago," we will reply, again nonchalantly.

But when we're alone, we break. The walls crumble. The doors come undone. Pain seeps into our veins and tears stream down our cheeks. We sit quietly. Alone. Away from the noise. From the watchful, misunderstanding eyes. We do not need anyone to tell us that it was so long ago. We know that. But that doesn't stop the pain. That doesn't lessen our heartache. It doesn't make us feel any better. We still feel the way we feel. We can't help it.

But maybe someday, after we've fought this war for long enough, we can raise the flag of victory. On it, will be our smiles. The kingdoms inside us will once again rejoice. Joy and peace will exit their hiding places. Triumph will dance in the streets. And love will reclaim every space of our healing hearts.

A Righteous Truth

Sometimes, we let go of the people we love. The moments and the memories our hearts cling to. And we do so because we care. We know that we are restricting them from the warmth and the enjoyment they deserve.

Pieces of us will die. But new memories, and new love, will heal our wounds. We are replenished in knowing that our humanity never dies. That we will always maintain our compassion for the betterment of the world.

Maybe I Do Have Trust Issues

There are so many things that occur inside me. But I don't show them. Because every time I do, people flee. As if my emotions are a tsunami coming to collapse their towns.

They head for the hills, and I'm left in the dust of their absence, wondering if they'll return. If they'll ever come back and apologize. Not even verbally, but with a quiet letter slipped beneath my door.

Thank You for Everything

I thought I'd never love again. My insides were wilting, and the petals spoke the name of every woman I failed to love. Until you emerged. Until the blinding light of your smile flooded the hallways of my heart. Until your name was inscribed on my rib cages.

You have shown me that I'm not broken. That I can still love. That my heart is an endless adventurer waiting for someone to grab its hand and take it on a wild journey.

No More

Stop thinking about it. Stop rereading old messages. Stop looking at their pictures and their new followers on social media. Walk away from the ledge you've been standing on in hopes of their return. Find your way back to you. Give yourself the love, the voice, and the attention you've deprived it of. Because there's a new life awaiting you. And it needs you to look forward to embrace it.

It'll Always Be You

Other women knock. But I do not answer. I have no interest in making my heart a home for them. It is a home for you.

Stay here. Bring your bags. I don't care what monsters crawl out, or what insecurities you harbor. I care about you. I know this journey is draining. But I'm willing to commit to it. I'm willing to make it work. Nothing great comes easy. Therefore, I don't expect you to come easy. I expect to fight for you.

And I will. With everything in me. If this battlefield breaks my heart and robs me of everything I own, I'll depart gladly knowing that I fought with everything I have. Because you're worth it. Even when you run away. Even when you doubt the validity of my love. When you think you can't handle it.

I am here for you. The light that will never dim. The flower that smiles and bestows its scent. The star that shines and admires your splendor.

I am not going anywhere. And when you decide to stay, you will find the door wide open. I will not have changed the locks. Nor will I demand a passcode. You can enter, as if you've never left. With everything in place. The pictures on the wall. The TV playing your favorite show. And me standing there, waiting to love you all over again.

Samples of Heaven

I expected the night to end early. I'd walk you to your car, hug you before you got in, and thank you for a fun time.

But you then expressed words that every heart wants to hear: "Stay. We can sit in my car and talk for a little." I entered your car, a bookbag and bottles strewn across its floor. I knew you'd be paranoid about them, thinking that I'd deem you "messy."

But I didn't. I love seeing the private glimpses of your life. The little things that give me a preview of what goes on in that beautiful, rambunctious mind. I can't help but wonder if that backpack possesses a laptop storing all of your deepest thoughts. Or if those bottles were tossed aside and forgotten during one of your busy, chaotic days.

Yet I say nothing. I merely reassure you that your car isn't "messy," and that my room is far worse. You will never understand the elation I receive in getting to know you more. In getting deeper into your character.

Most men want to find themselves deep in a woman's body; but I want to find myself deep in your soul. Deep in the secrets that no hands have ever touched. I want to show you that, while life is difficult and while these situations offer an indescribable fragility, I am here. I am going to fight for you. For this. And for everything that I know we could be.

I Wanted to Show You More

I know that I often seem distracted while I'm with you. I'm sorry. I'm trying to absorb every minute you grant me. But it's hard to be fully present, when I can't escape your beauty and the sound of my thumping heart. When my mind keeps wondering if you'll be my greatest love story, or my biggest heartbreak.

Learning the Hard Way

Dear heart,

I'm sorry for hurting you. I've placed you in burning buildings. Told you that the fire was small, and there was still a chance to extinguish it. But I knew that the flames wouldn't depart without burning me for my foolishness.

I've placed you in lairs of wolves disguised as sheep. Even when you warned me, I disagreed and said that we needed to be more open. That we had been misled in the past. I can't fully blame myself, though. A part of growth is experiencing new moments and pushing ourselves. However, I should take your feelings more seriously. Thank you for never leaving me, and for always picking up the pieces that I break.

It Came from Within

I want to continue being patient. I love being in your life. I love witnessing your smile. Seeing your dimples. Your kind eyes and your soft lips. The tiny frame that walks gleefully toward everything.

But I don't want my patience to obligate you to me. I want you to choose me because you want me. Because I stir your soul. Not because you feel like you owe me something. You don't owe me anything. I don't know where this will go, but I can tell you that I'm here until the end. Until you decide to cut the rope. I will fall, but I will be content.

Some moments are meant to be fleeting, night drives that are cut short because there's work in the morning. And you have been my favorite moment thus far. The chapter I'll read endlessly, in hopes of a beautiful ending.

Maybe Now, You'll Understand How I See You

Seeing you every time feels like the first time. Nerves rush through me, and my heart continuously asks the same question: "When will she be ours?"

But she is not mine. Nor is she yours. She is hers. She is the world's. She belongs to every Californian mountaintop. To every sunset and every beautiful shore. To every cloud that invites planes to soar through. To every adventurous path with new sights. And she must remain free.

September 29th, 2019

September 29th. That was the day I realized I was in love with you. The stadium was raucous, blue jerseys on every side. Yet all I noticed was you. Your cute dimples guarding your precious, infectious smile. Your curious gaze observing my every move.

It was the day I finally expelled all doubts and reservations and told myself to pursue you, fully and confidently. The conversation was great, your laughter and your sarcasm permeating my ears. I wanted to pull you in and hold you for a brief moment. I knew that I may never get the chance again, and I wanted to experience the warmth of your frame pressed against me. The love that could be shared and enjoyed in that fleeting moment, the way stunning scenery flies by a speeding car.

You made me realize that my heart can still love. That it still has so much affection. Perhaps that was your purpose. And now that it has been fulfilled, I'm unsure of what will happen. If you'll stay, or if you'll depart. But I am sure that I love you. With everything in me. With a heart that will never tire of your name. A mind that will work to honor you. And a soul that will live for your joy, even if it means sacrificing my own.

A Perfect Summer Day

So,
I have OCD.
It is so hard for me to sit
and simply enjoy
a woman's company.
As her radiant smile is before me
and the scent of coffee fills my nose,
my mind is working like a
machine.
What is she thinking
what am I doing here
how am I going to be with her
in a few years
am I really enjoying this
oh shit,
the conversation is starting to die
down and these thoughts are getting
louder—
but then I force myself to
stop.
Breathe.
Live in the moment.
I am with a beautiful woman,
and I want to take her in
the way
skin
takes in sweet sunlight.
And I do.

We walk around downtown Detroit
with cars zooming by
lights flashing
bikes speeding down sidewalks
and others filling the streets and laughing
loudly—but I notice only
her,
freckles dotting her cute cheeks
that my lips yearn to press themselves against
so that I can implant love into her core.
Her hair is light brown,
sand that can spill down my fingers
and carry my wishes into the winds of tomorrow.
Eventually, my mind is
eased.
Peace is upon me.
We are sitting on a bench near a fire station,
sunlight adorning her soft, tender skin.
The conversation is flowing like a calming river.
And this is what makes
the thoughts
the struggling
the OCD
and the mental storms worth it:
the quiet moments where I can feel the pure bliss
of being fully
immersed
in another individual.
Feeling her words.
Breathing the same air.
And indulging in the energetic conversation.
The sun sets and then I see the most
picturesque scene:
her sitting there,
a subtle smile on her face,

her curious, penetrating gaze
digging itself deeply into my eyes
and into my heart.
And if there is a heaven,
I hope it is an endless moment
of this.
Of being enveloped in uninhibited serenity.
Of watching both inward and outward beauty.
Of being content with simply another person's
company, and nothing more.

Open Yourself

Your heart
is as
deep
as the ocean,
yet you entertain
those
who only walk
along
its shores.

No Guarantees

Love is ever-changing. And sometimes, it outgrows us. It desires different scenery and different opportunities. Ultimately, love enters and love leaves.

And if it goes, we must let go gracefully. Change doesn't guarantee that love and people will stay; but it does guarantee that, with the right amount of effort and work, we will end up where we desire.

Is It Someday Yet?

Someday, you'll get tired of feeling worthless. Feeling alone. Feeling neglected and like you're a bother. And you'll realize that you're better off moving on. You'll look back. You'll reminisce on the good times.

But you need to make a distinction between your mind and reality. Because you can't invest yourself in potential. You need to invest yourself in certainty. In the people and the things who match your efforts.

Another One of Life's Great Lessons

Maybe we needed them to break our hearts, so that we could finally learn to let go and love ourselves.

Loving You Eternally

Even if every inch of you is
swallowed
by flames,
I will be there
to gather
the ashes.

No More Judgment

To understand
another person,
you must swim
in the same waters
that drowned them.

Give Them a Chance

Don't incarcerate another for a crime they didn't commit. Don't make them fight for your trust, and for your love, because someone else hurt you. They are not that person.

Nor can they be expected to carry those burdens. Keep your heart open, and remember that most people are good. They just need to learn how to love.

When Will You See It's Yours?

My heart is
open
for you.
A door your soft feet can walk
through.
Run your hands
across
its walls
and feel
my love
in all its
beats.

It Still Hurts

What a loss it is,
to bid farewell
to someone
you swore
would be your
forever.

I Didn't Want to Go

It hurts to let go. But it hurts to stay somewhere you don't belong. In a place that chains you. A place that prevents you from receiving the warmth and the love you're worthy of.

Someday, You'll Understand

It's hard withholding all my feelings. I fear my expressions will send you away. That you will take the first chance to throw your love, your effort, and your happiness into a suitcase and run off.

I wish I could tell you how important you are to me. How thankful I am that we have grown in new ways. But these words are the monsters you run from. They ravage your insides and unearth all the skeletons you've buried.

Still, I want to spend more time with you. I want to look into your eyes. Count the freckles on your cheeks. See the way you react to a funny joke when your mouth is full. Listen to the way your heart flutters when I hold your hand. But these privileges are restricted from my heart. A heart that begs to conjoin with yours.

And someday, you'll understand that my love wasn't a mirage, but a gift that I knew you were worthy of.

An Honest Realization

Love has taught me that I'm still insecure and impatient. I still get jealous and I can be codependent. I want to be a person's number one. Their everything. The force they can rely on to sweep their troubles away.

But I constantly remind myself that the world is greater than me. It has countless places to visit and endless forces conspiring for innumerable events. I can't expect to outshine and overpower them. I am a speck on the world's surface. And I will accept a smaller role and acknowledge that every individual occupies a certain space with their own path.

It's All OK

A part of growing is feeling. Acknowledge your hurt. Pick the shrapnel from your heart. Forgive yourself for the times you knew better and went ahead anyway. It's all OK. And it's all necessary to become the person you want to be.

I Didn't Want to Leave

If you want to leave, leave. I'm exasperated with this process. The coming. The going. The pleading for answers. The mixed, indeterminable emotions.

But know this: had you been willing to fight for us, we could have made it work. Because I never would have left your side. All you had to do was utter one simple word: "stay." And there I would have been, waiting for you with open arms and a kind smile.

Give Me Substance

I don't care about the pretty faces. The nice bodies. The colored eyes. Show me substance. Show me lips that speak kind words and a heart that beats to honor them. Hands that toil daily to build a better world. Legs that walk to offer comfort to ailing souls.

I desire the people who have depth. The people who stand against the odds to fight, regardless of the outcome. But I only see shallowness; faces that don't care and bodies that scurry off for self-preservation. Give me the people who give a damn. The people who will suspend their happiness to lend consolation to others.

Maybe "The One" is Real After All...

People tell me I fall easily. Normally, I'd agree. But not when it pertains to you. Not when you are everything I've been seeking.

You have the perfect smile. It's a living canvas I never tire of. Your eyes see me in ways many others do not. They are scanners detecting all my good and raising my eagerness to change the bad. Your mind is a stunning universe. There is so much to navigate.

Don't cut my journey short. I will stay here for as long as you'll have me. You are the prophecy I was told about love. The one woman who has shown me why the fairytales aren't so farfetched. Why there is still a reason to believe.

Do You Finally Understand?

I will prove to you that I love you, even if you have to trample my heart. That I'm here for you, even if you walk away. That I'll fight for you, even if you reject my love.

Nothing will keep me from you. Not even death. I will bow to God's throne and beg him to return me to you. I will be the air that wafts through your soft skin. The sunlight that dances upon your sweet freckles. The flowers that beckon to you in the distance. The random smiling stranger that reminds you of the world's beauty. I will live on in you, the heart that gave me a home. The heart that I will eternally love.

Maybe You'll Finally Understand

Love is beautiful. But it hurts when our lovers leave. When they traverse new borders without us. When new hands overtake theirs and new lips stir wonder inside them.

You are not only my love, but my biggest fear: I am petrified of the pain your departure will bring. Of the hurt dangling before me. I know it's only a matter of time until my fears become a reality. Until they manifest as the ghosts that'll haunt my worn heart.

Outside of your flaws—the very things I can eerily, and strangely, overlook—you are everything I've been seeking. You ferment my desire to be great. With you, I am a superhero saving his princess. I am empowered to slay any demon. Nothing daunts me; your love is the gravity that keeps my body grounded.

And your smile is a constellation I never tire of. I keep finding new ways to outline it in the sky. And when I see it, I point and say, "That's my compass. The light that guides me home."

Full Surrender

I will no longer deny reality. I will accept the truth. And the truth is that I will always expect more. The same way the sun expects the flowers to bloom and prosper from its light and its warmth, is the same way that I will expect my love for you to place me into your future.

I cannot help that I have fallen madly for you. That I am, without your knowledge, yours. I lock the door and barricade myself from other women and contemplate you in every opportunity. The universe could offer me the best job and infinite happiness elsewhere, and all I'd contemplate is if you're a part of its plan. If your smile will grace my horizon, and if your touch will be the only one I'll know.

This Hurt the Most

No matter how much I gave,
it was never enough.
It made me feel
worthless.
I was trying to be the path that'd take you
everywhere
you wanted to go—and that was the problem:
I never realized this meant that
you'd have to
walk
all
over
me.

Trust in Your Healing

Some days, your heart will break all over again.
This is how it will heal and empty itself of pain.

You Did Your Part

You gave them everything you could. It's time to walk away and reclaim yourself. To pour your love into your heart and to allow yourself to bloom.

Part Three:
The Becoming

I Finally Opened Myself to Love; to You

For once, everything makes sense. The butterflies. The fears. The dispersion of ego. It's all falling into place, raindrops descending quietly upon the Earth. I know they're watering the beautiful path that she and I will walk on, our hands interlaced.

Our hearts will converge, and love will be born. It will be the fulfillment of a promise I've long awaited. The culmination that'll make sense of every failure we've endured. And I promise that I will make her the happiest individual on the planet.

As You Are, Always

I don't care about your past. Because I like you. Every piece of you. Even the pieces that are cracked, chipped, and faded. The pieces that you try to hide.

I will find them. Not to shame you. But to love you, and value you, in your entirety. There is nothing to hide. But there is a future to build. And it starts with using the pieces of our pasts to better understand one another, and to form tomorrow's foundation.

I Accept This, Too

I have realized that departure is in your nature. Before, I took everything personally. It had to be my inadequacy that was pushing you towards the border. My inner deficiencies that you couldn't live with.

But I realized that it was beyond me. And many things are beyond than me. We get so caught up in our lives, that we forget about the worlds within others. The worlds that contain pains, nightmares, and secrets.

I am sorry for taking things personally. I just wanted to be there. To hold you during your storms and to wipe your tears. But some issues transcend me, and I cannot force my way in.

It's You, and I Wish You'd See That

You have already cheated every woman who tries to get close to me. You have stolen pieces of my heart, and my soul, that I can never give to them. Pieces they will ask about.

And when they question why I'm inattentive, or why my heart is fragmented, I will avoid answering. But you will ring in my mind. A distant voice I will yearn to hear once more. Soft hands I'll wish to hold. You are the answer, and my heart will always roam the borders of what we could have been.

Maybe This is What You Need

You're much happier when you're away. When you're not interacting with me. When there isn't the pressure of having to confront your feelings.

And if I love you, I must leave. I can't stick around knowing that you're going to be unhappy with where this is headed. Knowing that, as more feelings emerge, more of your discomfort does, too. I want you to be content. Even if it means that I must roam the borders of your heart without ever being permitted entry.

So, this is farewell. To you. To our story. To the potential that flashed in your eyes.

I will miss you. My heart will be flooded with your memories and I will be submerged. But your happiness will be the life preserver that I will cling to. It will guide me back to the shores. And someday, I'll be thankful for making the decisions that shattered my heart countless times.

Tell Them About Me

One day, when your hair is grayer, and wrinkles are sitting beneath those curious eyes that I once gazed into, your grandchildren will be asking you about love.

And I hope that you remember me. I hope that my hand protrudes beneath the ground that you buried me under. That my words flash in your mind, and butterflies soar wildly in your stomach. I want to know that all of this meant more. That what we had wasn't an illusion. That you and I were a real love story. And that, even after many years, a heart still burns for the love that ignited it.

Rest Easy, My Memories

I'm finding happiness. The old memories don't prey on me. My skin is healing, and the scars don't whisper at night. The names that once haunted me have been buried peacefully. I do not mourn at their gravesites. I place flowers of gratitude. I smile and I thank them for the memories. For the moments and the times that birthed who I am.

It Wasn't Me

I have finally realized
that I was
enough
all along.
It was they who were
broken
and unable to realize
my value.

Missed Opportunities

When I'm lying on my
deathbed,
I will not reflect on the
love that I gave,
but on the
beautiful moments that I
squandered
as I awaited their
endings.

Show Me All of You

I don't know your favorite color yet. Nor do I know your favorite restaurant. But I do know that your eyes hold forever in them, and that your heart calls to me. You've defined my meaning of home; it is in your warm embrace.

You're Never as Bad as You Think You Are

I was unable to forgive myself. Unable to move on and accept that sometimes, we are the ones who hurt others. The ones who pull the triggers, and who detonate the bridges that we loved crossing. The ones who pack people's bags and send them away.

I replayed our final day endlessly. It was a horror film my mind couldn't escape. I was the villain. The one who broke a heart, and who never made proper reparations.

But then I realized I wasn't a villain. Villains are greedy and hurtful. Often arrogant and malicious. But I was none of those to you. I left because I wanted what was best for you. I wanted your heart to roam freely. Not to be tethered to an uncertain individual. This realization was the key that unlocked my chains. The liberation I had been awaiting. And I hope you find happiness. I hope you heal.

Forever Loving You

When I die,
I wish to be
reincarnated as the ocean's
shores.
I know that's where I'll find
you,
sitting alongside me,
a book in your hands and a smile
etched through your face.

Love is Unconditional, Thanks to You

You have taught me that love is unconditional. You could burn my reality. Tear my heart out and stomp on it. Hurl insults at me.

And I will still love you. I will clutch the image of your smiling face tightly to my heart. Lose myself in your dimples and in your curious, all-seeing eyes.

Time can change you. Misfortune can arise. But you will forever be the woman cheering with me at Lions games. The woman who sings softly during her favorite concerts. And the woman whose passion for life awakens the man in me I've always dreamed of becoming.

Let Yourself Bloom

Forgive yourself. Let the past go. Wave goodbye as it sails in the distance. See your new self in the splashing waves. See the sun's radiance overhead.

Not every ending is an ending. It is a beginning. A chance to rebuild. A chance to mold yourself. And a chance to find beauty in new places and in new people.

To Survivors of Abuse:

I'm sorry it happened. I'm sorry demons visit you nightly, as the rest of your household is asleep. That tears cover your eyes and block the light that's trying to reach you. That you can't enjoy interpersonal relationships and falling in love.

But it's not over. The story is still being written. And your hands are strong enough to write its final chapter. Don't let pain, fear, and agony be its authors. You can give your character a smile and a brighter outlook. And you can heal.

Though we carry the baggage of abuse around with us, we don't have to stop our flights. At each new destination, we can open our luggage and leave something behind. And soon, it will be empty. It'll have room for new memories, new moments, and new items of joy.

We aren't victims; we are survivors. We will pass the torch onto new generations. We will empower their struggling voices. We will dig through the rubble, pick them up, and encourage them to heal. We may be feeling hurt. Broken. Defeated. But we aren't dead. Time is still ticking. The universe is still expanding. And we are still rising, no matter how hard it gets.

Maybe Love Isn't What We Think

Love is not a permanent feeling of bliss and joy. Sometimes, it's average. Quiet and calm, a breeze wafting through a meadow. It is soft. A gentle petal caressing our fingertips. Love is a star: always present, no matter how far we go. And it will guide us home.

Self-Gratitude

I want to thank the pain that agonized me during lonely nights. It made me more compassionate. The abuse that was inflicted upon me at a young age. It forced my skin to grow armor, so that I could become a warrior. The women who left me. Their departures helped me discover who I wanted to be.

And lastly, I want to thank myself. For never giving up. For continuously rising. For loving consistently, no matter how many my heart has been broken. For believing in the good of the world, no matter how many bullets rip through the air or how many bodies fill the graves. For making the right decisions, irrespective of the pain I feel. And for standing firmly on life's shores as society's conspiring waves bash against me.

These experiences have made me the man I am today. And nothing will take that from me.

Keep Believing

Remember: there were good moments before this pain. Moments that forged the biggest smile on your face, and that showered your heart with love. And they'll return. Only this time, with all the lessons you've learned, they'll be better.

It Always Works Out

I've made mistakes. I've walked away too soon. Said the wrong things. Drawn tears out of undeserving eyes. Shattered hearts—and those broken pieces still slice through me. Stomped on emotions, and put myself ahead when I shouldn't have.

But I wouldn't change anything. I am proud of the compassionate, kind person I've become. And he wouldn't be here without the mistakes that led the way.

The Truth About Love

We've been lied to about love. It's not at first sight. Nor the butterflies. The intense nerves and the rushing excitement.

Love is a process. It involves exploration. Honesty. A willingness to overcome problems. A desire to sift through another's murky waters to find the treasures beneath.

And so many of us are empty, lacking love and searching endlessly, because we're looking for the wrong traits. In the wrong places. With the wrong people.

Fall in love with the process of growing together. With overcoming your common struggles. With uplifting one another. With being one another's source of strength, when either of you are struggling.

Because love is not a destination. It is an endless journey. A deep exploration of one's self, as we learn to conjoin with another.

Letting Go Gracefully

People tell me things about you, expecting a reaction. Expecting hate to flash in my eyes. Anger to spew from my lips.

And they're surprised when it's the opposite. When kindness flashes in my eyes, and gratitude spills from my lips. I do not hate you. I do not resent you. Even if I'm not in your life, you're still in my mind. Wrapped in my warmest thoughts. Covered in my best wishes.

There is no need for bitterness. To wish misfortune upon you. We didn't work out. And that's OK. The sun is still rising. The world is still revolving. You're still fulfilling your routines and moving forward.

And if you need anything, I am here. I am never out of reach. I may be distant, but I'm watching over you, always.

Tomorrow Will Come

I've been sitting in my head lately. Looking at past pictures. Seeing old friends, lovers, and dreams. Some are kindled; quiet fires that keep me warm. Others are collecting dust. I look away. It hurts to face certain moments. To relive the pain. To see that smiles have turned into frowns. That once-beating hearts have stopped and shattered.

But sunlight creeps through the window. Tomorrow is on the horizon. He tells me that everything is going to be OK. That I don't have to worry. That someday, life won't be as dark. New opportunities, new company, and new moments will knock on my door. And by then, I'll be ready.

Don't Dive in If You Can't Swim

A friend told me that I have "too much depth." That not many will be able to swim in these waters. My thoughts? Don't.

The Pacific Ocean welcomes the finest, strongest ships to enter. Not the flimsy ships. The ones that disintegrate at the sight of a storm.

I am the same. If you cannot handle the depths of these waters, don't enter. There are no shallow ponds. No kiddy pools, either. These waters are vast and filled with wonder below.

And if others are unwilling to handle the depth, it is their loss. Not mine. I want those who can marvel at all that I am. Those who are willing to share their depth with me. And anyone who's timid, is doing me a favor by leaving.

There is Still a Chance

Nothing is worse than heartache. You sever ties that you spent years building. You walk away from a dream. A seemingly endless journey. You swore your hands would be interlaced forever, and that your finger would end up with a ring upon it. A commitment that would last eternally. And when you have to bid farewell to these long-harbored dreams, a piece of you dies. You lose who you once were.

But it's never the end. You're still alive, and blank pages are awaiting you. Grab a pen and start writing. Give your life's book new chapters. Fill them with new characters and plentiful opportunities to love and to heal. To grow and to offer salvation. Pain hurts, but it is the cocoon holding our growth. And just as the butterfly emerges, we will, too.

And Sometimes, it Still Hurts

I spoke to you recently. It felt like ages. Time was frozen. Trapped in the moment when we were together. When I'd visit you every day. Spend hours at your apartment. Play with our cat, as the aroma of your food wafted through the room.

It's all so vivid. A portrait affixed to my mind. Even when I cover it, I still hear the voices. Your sorrow calls to me, and my sorrow responds. We are, even in our distance, welded together by pain. By a common desire to emerge through the heartache.

Your voice is still the same: soft. Kind. Gentle. Wind that brushes down a perspired back during a hot summer day. Your ears are still angels that wish to carry my problems away. You listened to my feelings the same way you always did: openly. Ready to absorb them. Even if you don't have a remedy. But I've since realized that listening ears are a remedy. Thank you for yours.

We caught up. Talked about work. Your family. School and your finances. You asked me about my grandma. You were surprised to hear that she still asks about you, too. About how things are going and if you're happy.

I told you that I, too, want you happy. I was elated when you expressed to me that you've been going out again. I hope that the sunlight and the winds brush through your worn face. That your tired hands are renewed as different opportunities enter them. Keep living. Thrive. Move on from the chains of your past. You deserve the happiness you've been seeking.

Overall, it was a refreshing conversation. The closure we both needed. Even though you didn't want to hear my full apology. I understand. Words cut through the stitches. I need to let your wounds heal more. Because mine are still healing. I realized that when we ended the phone call. I ran to the bathroom, turned on the shower, and wept. Tears burst through my eyes. Landslides of sorrow finally tumbling down. Finally setting my struggles free.

The sound of your voice, and the duration of that phone call, echoed our past. The way we'd talk for hours and get through the roughest days. Now, we get through them without each other. Without your soft ears and my reassuring voice.

And I will remember you. In the tenderest ways. In the kindest moments. I hope you remember me in the same manner. Not as I left, but as I entered and helped. Not as I lost my temper, but as I held you during the hardest nights. Not as we cried, but as we grew and loved.

You are woven in my heart. A fine thread that I will show my grandchildren, the way others show their shining awards. We may not have realized it then, but I'm certain we do now: we loved each other, in ways we were unaware of. And for that, I am thankful. For that, I will always remember you.

What Love Really Entails

We spend so much time trying to force love to magically appear, that we miss out on the very moments that forge it. The late-night car rides. The long phone conversations. The dinner dates and the concerts. We live in our heads, and we forget to indulge in the moment. To dip our hands into the present's sweetness. To lay beside the ocean of calm beckoning to us.

Then, we let our lovers go. They walk into the sunset, taking their bags of good treatment and admiration with them. We tell ourselves that we "deserve better." That we "weren't feeling it." That they should have invoked more in us. Then, their absence descends upon us, darkness spreading throughout the night sky.

And we feel it all: the feelings that had been brewing. The enjoyment we grew accustomed to. The familiarity that unlocked our inner gates.

Suddenly, love floods us. We realize that it was there. The entire time. With every smile exchanged, and every bit of laughter shared. We were falling without realizing it. If only we would have been more present. We would have realized that what we were seeking, was always there.

Maybe This is Goodbye

You know you've moved on when you can listen to the saddest songs, and your eyes stay clear. When you can see their pictures, and your heart doesn't break. When you can hear their voice, and no angry demons march to your mind's borders.

And when you can genuinely, and sincerely, wish them well. You're able to close the book for the final time and hope that life is treating them kindly. That the paths they're embarking on are filled with smiling faces, warm hands, and loving hearts.

Unsaid Words

"You promised me you wouldn't leave."

"And I meant it. But that was when I thought my feelings mattered to you. I can't stay in a place where my feelings are neglected. Where everything is on someone else's terms. I matter, too. My feelings, my thoughts, and my desires matter. And if they won't be treated meaningfully, I'll respect myself enough to leave."

We'll Always Remember

I wish I would have immersed myself deeper in you. I regret squandering hours in my head during our dates. Still, there was much I enjoyed.

Like the time we trekked the path in Ford Field. Leaves sprawled throughout the ground. Mud clinging to the bottom of my high-tops. Mosquitos ravaging our skin.

I slung you over my shoulders and told you to hang on. I walked with you attached to my back, your laughter ringing in the background. Your warm breath rushing through my neck.

I then made you do an impromptu photoshoot. You sat atop the bridge's ledge, sunlight gleaming in your then-blonde hair. Water streaming in the background. It was a sample of heaven. A sweetness I couldn't get enough of.

And a part of my spirit still roams that bridge, watching younger you and younger me. Smiling at all that we were, and at the growth awaiting us.

My Promise to You

It's important to remember that pain is temporary. Anger leaves. Jealousy subsides. And we come back to ourselves. We realize that these problems were never that big. That we are far worthier than the half-hearted attempts people offered us. And that we grow in unimaginable ways, and we become shining versions of ourselves we never thought possible.

So, don't give up. Hang on. Fight to return to the top. This is all temporary. A journey that you must endure and persevere through. And you will make it.

Stop The Hate And The Bitterness

Someone posted a Facebook status asking what advice one would offer to their ex's new partner. The answers were hateful and bitter. "I'd tell her to run away while she still can," one person wrote. "Be prepared to deal with a lot of nagging," another wrote.

I can't be sure of what happened in these relationships. Maybe abuse occurred. Or maybe there was a horrific ending. But I can say what advice I'd have for my ex's new partner.

Please, be good to her. Shower her with love, with affection, and with care. Offer her a tender heart to rest in. Her sarcasm is like wine: it gets better with time. Be grateful for her listening ear. None can absorb your words better than she does. None can provide a safe space for communication like her. The couch you're sitting on becomes a pair of hands that hold you. The air becomes an open path, and everything flows smoothly.

Make sure you love her, before it's too late. Before time gives you an eviction notice, and you find yourself wandering the future's plains alone. Wishing you would have said more. Wishing you would have done more. Reminiscing on the nights you held her, and she kissed your cheeks. On the long outings where you took her hand and felt its warmth permeate your body.

I was fortunate to experience such kindness and goodness. I was able to see that love can be safe and welcoming. That I can lower my inner walls and accept what I'm worthy of. And all of us can make such realizations, once we let go of the anger and the bitterness.

Ultimately, you should be grateful, if you've experienced a good relationship and a respectable ending. You're walking away with growth and a stronger foundation.

I know it hurts. I know your heart mourns on silent, lonesome nights. I know you spend time alone to prevent others from seeing your tears. But amid all this pain, love exists. And it's a love that showed you how capable you are and how beautiful life is. A love that highlighted your heart's strength and its ability to feel beyond what you thought was possible.

Hope

You didn't need to be perfect. Nor did you need to sleep with me. I didn't want you to tell me everything, or for you to make me the center of your universe. I only wanted you to meet me halfway on this bridge. For you to end this one-sided loneliness. And just as I expressed this, you walked away. But before you disappeared, you raised your hand and pushed the button, detonating the bridge. Destroying any hope I harbored. Any belief that we may meet here again.

But I believe that life has more than one pathway. More than one route to reach our destination. If one bridge is destroyed, we can find, or build, another one.

Maybe I wasn't meant to cross this bridge with you. Maybe we're meant to meet at a different one, at a different time. Where you'll be transparent and more expressive. And I'll be healed and more prepared.

And maybe this time, we won't have to meet in the middle. Maybe we'll be on the same side, crossing it together. Entering love's borders to a welcoming party beneath a clear, sunny sky. And laughing at how silly it was to have drifted apart in the first place.

The Hard Truth

It hurts when people walk away. It cracks our hearts, and pain spills atop everything. Like the other opportunities that come our way. We distrust newcomers and place them on a crucifix of old lovers' sins. We tell them that they must surpass our newly built obstacle courses. They must run through the plains of our heartache. Climb the mountains of our pain. Go deep into the wilderness and gather five pieces of love, two handfuls of apologies, and three buckets full of our self-worth, and rebuild our trust.

Then, we wonder why they flee. Why they fail to deliver on our knowingly unrealistic expectations. We'll call them "scared." "Unwilling." "Afraid of commitment." But we'll never criticize ourselves. We'll never realize that we are the exact things we accuse them of being. And it's all because we yearn for their entry, but we're too afraid of getting hurt.

The Only Way

Love so fully,
that people
will always carry
a piece of you
wherever
they go.

A Universal Promise

And believe me,
if it is meant for
you,
it will find you
again.

Across the Border

My heart is across
the border,
I say.
And they look at me
like I'm mad.
"You walk funny; you slur your words."
I reproach them and say that none
can function with their body in
shambles.
Still, they look at me, confused.
My heart is across
the border,
I say.
It's there. I hear its cries.
And I cannot liberate it.
My heart is across
the border
searching
seeking
pleading
and vying for the love
it has lost:
her.
A smile so luminous,
they could name it a new star;
chestnut hair
that cascades
down her shoulders,

a waterfall
washing the sorrow
off fingertips.
My heart is across the border,
I say.
Please, if you cross,
search for
it.
Tell it that I am in need,
and that it is OK to move on.
To let her
go.
My heart is across
the border,
I say.
Because that is where
it has found its
home.

I Know the Real You

Your heart is not
barren
the way others believe.
It is fertile.
Filled with
multi-colored flowers
and vast forests.
In it,
I have planted
my dreams.
And when they
bloom,
promise me you will water them.
Promise me you will seek me
in the petals of every
unsaid word.
In the quiet spaces
of shade.
You will see me in all things.
And you will then understand
the love
I have for you.

Always Love Deeply

People say having a deep heart is a curse. I disagree. I pity those who will never be able to experience love the way I do. The love that overtakes my soul. That courses through my veins. That clothes me in strength and baptizes me in humility. It may bring waves of pain; but it always leaves me in an ocean of fulfillment.

Memories Are OK

And I will remember.
The way your hands
gripped mine,
a smile carved through your cheeks.
The way your hair cascaded
down your
shoulders,
my fingers running through it.
Your sweet voice
that reverberated
through my mental forest—
even the trees
swayed
to the sound of your
name.
The lips that
kissed me
like a tide kissing the shore.
The sunlight meant more
back then.
Now, I am a mummified corpse
awaiting your love to
unwrap me.
To rescue me from this sarcophagus
of misery.
No eternal resting place should be devoid
of love.

Do not send me to
purgatory.
That is a life without your love.

No Shame in Being Human

Everyone makes mistakes.
It is how we
rise
after the
fall
that defines us.

An Honest Expression

I fell for
you.
For your smile. Your freckles.
Your wondrous, vast mind
filled
with intricate secrets and details.
I am an explorer and
you
are the
new world.
I will take an expedition and journey through
your deep heart.
Run through its wide fields.
Search through its mazes.
Meditate in its temples.
Walk through your forests and
carve
my name
in
every tree.
Indeed,
I love you
deeply,
because there is
no other
way.

We Always Grow

Some goodbyes
emerge
with hollow footsteps.
We leave our love
in
their imprints.
Some goodbyes
emerge
through the broken pieces of our hearts.
Still, we carry on.
We march through the darkness,
the unchartered territory of loss
which leads to
self-discovery.
And some goodbyes
are too painful to remember.
So we tuck them away.
Lock them in our mind's attic
and recollect them only when asked.
But all goodbyes
are new beginnings
that wipe our tears,
so that we may see
the future's impending
smiles
and its
open palms.

And I Have Finally Learned

I disbelieved that love was unconditional. I thought I had to be funnier. Wiser. Fitter and taller. It was so hard to believe that I could be loved, merely for who I was. Merely for this flesh and blood that carried so much inner brokenness.

But so many were willing to venture into my deepest depths and shower them in love. In praise. Admire them in awe. Question why my heart still possesses certain relics, and what the stories are regarding its fractures.

And I realized that I must replicate such kindness, by dispelling my own misapprehensions. I loved others conditionally, because that's what was modeled to me. And it was difficult to believe that I was recreating the same painful patterns.

So, I changed. I ripped down my old mental posters. I renovated my older ideologies. Expelled doubt and hate. Invited more love in.

And this time, the love would be unconditional. A radiant lighthouse for all weary travelers sailing doubt's sea. I would love with no expectations. I would penetrate all inner walls with my utmost fervor and my boundless devotion, because that is the ultimate expression of unconditional love.

Thank you for reading, and supporting, my work. For more, follow my Instagram page, @ writingtoinspire, and subscribe to my podcast, "The Writing to Inspire Podcast," which is available on Apple, Google, Spotify, and any other app you use.

Acknowledgments:

I would like to thank God, the Creator and Sustainer of all existence. I am grateful for His Divine Alignment that has made my growth, and my achievements, possible.

Next, I can never overstate how fortunate I am to receive such an amazing amount of support from family, friends, and other communities.

To my dad: thank you for believing in me, and for allowing me to choose my own path. I appreciate your confidence in the man I've become.

To my grandma: I appreciate your unwavering love, support, and encouragement. You have always believed in me, and have taught me to push for what I desire.

To my aunt Cynthia and uncle Joe: I appreciate you both treating me like I'm one of your own. Your love and support have impacted me tremendously. Thank you.

To my brother, Jason: your kindness, your curiosity, and your loving spirit encourage me daily. I'm proud of you, and I'm lucky to have you on my side.

To the best cousins (who are basically my other siblings): Anthony, Erik, Jaclyn, Jessica, and Nadine: thank you all so much for always inspiring me and believing in me. You all are the greatest support system I can ask for. I am indebted to each of you. You have emboldened me, and supported my vision, since day one. Much love.

To my friends:

Javel: Thank you for always standing by me, no matter how dark it gets. You never fail to remind me about my greatness and my direction. You are one person I can always count on. Your insight has been my compass on many occasions. I appreciate you deeply.

Houda C.: Thank you for always guiding me and showing me my potential and my talents, irrespective of my struggles. I cherish your unwavering support and your commitment to my growth. You have supported me in many ways. For that, I am eternally thankful.

Abdullah A.: you've always highlighted my creativity and my determination. I am thankful for all of our discussions about my dreams and my hopes. Much appreciated.

Alex A.: Thank you for supporting me since we were in high school. I am truly fortunate to have such an encouraging, kind friend. You have always encouraged my writing goals. I hope you know how much I value you.

Hassan H.: From purchasing my novels, to listening to me vent, and always letting people know that I'm an author, I am deeply thankful. You inspire me in many ways. Thank you for being a great friend during some of my darkest times.

Hanan C.: Thank you for supplying me with a boundless amount of belief, encouragement, and inspiration. You have seen sides of my writing that none have. I am indebted to you for your kindness, your support, and your natural, all-encompassing spirit that has fueled not only a large part of this work, but also my life, my growth, and my heart. Words cannot fully articulate what you mean to me. I hope that now, you finally understand, and that it all has settled well within you.

Hassan A.: Thank you for being a constant source of inspiration and reassurance. I am lucky to have you in my life.

Firas H.: Thank you for teaching me, early on, to embrace my emotions. "How you feel is how you feel, J." Those words have stuck with me, and they inspired my growth infinitely.

Mohsen A: I deeply appreciate your kindness and support, especially during some of the roughest points in my life. I am lucky to have such a devoted friend. Thank you for being you.

Joe B.: Thank you for believing in me, and for always providing me with support, reassurance, and guidance. Your words have left a greater impact than you'll ever know.

Lastly, to the Writingtoinspire community: you all have transformed my life. I appreciate the endless stream of support, encouragement, and love. You all shower me in inspiration. This is for all of you. I am so humbled to have such a loving, inspiring community. Much love, and happy healing.

Made in the USA
Coppell, TX
06 May 2021